1 Introduction

Economists want their empirical results to be robust, and with good reason. Especially after Goldfeld's (1976) missing money and Lucas's (1976) critique, economists have been all too aware of the fragility of many empirical models to the choice of (e.g.) explanatory variables, sample period, and dynamics. In an attempt to measure a coefficient's sensitivity to model selection, Leamer's (1983) extreme bounds analysis (also known as sensitivity analysis) calculates the range of potential coefficient estimates over a class of models. Extreme bounds analysis thus offers an appealing and intuitive methodology for determining whether an empirical result is robust or fragile. Extreme bounds analysis also formalizes a common practice in empirical studies, and its explicit implementation is widespread; cf. Allen and Connolly (1989), Cooley and LeRoy (1981), Levine and Renelt (1992), Leamer (1997), Sala-i-Martin (1997), Serra (2006), Freille, Haque, and Kneller (2007), and Bjørnskov, Dreher, and Fischer (2008) *inter alia*.

Robustness and fragility in Leamer's sense are defined with respect to a particular coefficient or set of coefficients over a class of models. This paper shows that the inclusion of the data generation process in that class of models is neither necessary nor sufficient for robustness. This result holds even if the properly specified model has well-determined, statistically significant coefficients. The encompassing principle—pioneered by Mizon (1984) and Mizon and Richard (1986)—explains how this result can occur. Encompassing also provides a link to a more common-sense notion of robustness that *is* a desirable property empirically; and encompassing clarifies recent discussion on model averaging and the pooling of forecasts.

Put somewhat differently, extreme bounds analysis focuses on the variation of estimated coefficients across model specifications. While that coefficient variation is of interest, it is so only in light of its causes. Extreme bounds analysis considers *all* coefficient variation, regardless of its causes. The encompassing principle discerns between coefficient variation that is not explainable by the model at hand, and coefficient variation that is. Encompassing thus clarifies when to worry about coefficient variation and when not to, whereas extreme bounds analysis worries about all coefficient variation. In essence, extreme bounds analysis is not sensitive enough to the data's nuances, whereas the encompassing principle is.

Section 2 briefly describes extreme bounds analysis, including modifications proposed by Leamer and Leonard (1983) and Levine and Renelt (1992). Section 3 establishes the lack of necessity and the lack of sufficiency through illustrations with classical regression models. Section 4 demonstrates how robustness and fragility in Leamer's sense are themselves fragile in practice, employing Hendry and Ericsson's (1991) model of U.K. money demand. Section 5 re-interprets the fragility of sensitivity analysis in light of the encompassing principle. In so doing, Section 5 clarifies the meaning of robustness and illuminates recent discussion on model averaging and the pooling of forecasts. Section 6 concludes.

In order to make the results readily accessible, examples—rather than proofs—are employed. Also, proofs are readily apparent, given the examples.

2   A Characterization

This section summarizes extreme bounds analysis (EBA), including modifications proposed by Leamer and Leonard (1983) and Levine and Renelt (1992). The classical regression model serves to illustrate. See Leamer (1978, Chapter 5) for an initial discussion of Bayesian sensitivity analysis; and see Leamer and Leonard (1983), Leamer (1985), and Levine and Renelt (1992) for more detailed descriptions of EBA.

Consider the standard linear regression model:

$$y_t = x_t' \beta_F + z_t' \gamma + u_t \qquad u_t \sim IN(0, \sigma^2) \qquad t = 1, \dots, T, \qquad (1)$$

where y_t is the dependent variable, x_t and z_t are $k \times 1$ and $q \times 1$ vectors of "free" and "doubtful" explanatory variables, β_F and γ are $k \times 1$ and $q \times 1$ vectors of their coefficients, u_t is a normal independently distributed disturbance with mean zero and variance σ^2, and t is the time index for the interval $[1, T]$. A variable is free if *a priori* its coefficient is believed to be different from zero, and a variable is doubtful if *a priori* its coefficient is believed to be equal to zero.

Extreme bounds analysis centers on a "focus" coefficient, denoted β. Commonly, β is an element of β_F and so is associated with a free variable, although β could be any linear combination of $(\beta_F' : \gamma')$, as in Breusch (1990). Below, β is always an element of β_F, purely for expository convenience.

Extreme bounds analysis determines the range of the least squares estimates of β over variations in the set of doubtful variables z_t. To illustrate, consider equation (1) with two doubtful variables (z_{1t} and z_{2t}) and one free variable (x_t), where x_t is also the focus variable:

$$y_t = \beta x_t + \gamma_1 z_{1t} + \gamma_2 z_{2t} + u_t. \qquad (2)$$

Bounds can be calculated from the four estimates of β that are obtained by including or excluding each of the doubtful variables in equation (2). However, these bounds generally are not invariant to nonsingular linear transformations of the doubtful variables. For instance, a different set of bounds might arise if $z_{1t} - z_{2t}$ and z_{2t} (rather than z_{1t} and z_{2t}) were used as the doubtful variables.

Leamer and Leonard (1983) propose a simple solution to this conundrum: calculate the bounds over all linear combinations of the doubtful variables. While these bounds might appear complicated to compute, they are not; and Breusch (1990, equation (17)) provides analytical formulae for them in terms of standard regression output from (1), estimated with and without the restriction $\gamma = 0$. The bounds are:

$$\frac{\hat{\beta} + \tilde{\beta}}{2} \quad \pm \quad \frac{\left\{ \left[ese(\hat{\beta})^2 - (\hat{\sigma}^2/\tilde{\sigma}^2)ese(\tilde{\beta})^2 \right] qF_D \right\}^{1/2}}{2}, \quad (3)$$

where the circumflex ^ and tilde ~ denote unrestricted and restricted estimates respectively, $ese(\cdot)$ is the estimated standard error, and F_D is the F-statistic for testing the exclusion of all q doubtful variables. Below, these bounds are called $\beta_{\min}$ and $\beta_{\max}$. As Breusch notes, these bounds are narrow when exclusion of the doubtful variables results in either little loss of fit (F_D is small) or little change in the precision of the estimate of β when adjusted for possible changes in error variance. See Stewart (1984) for an alternative approach.

Estimation of β is "robust" if the range of inferences about β is small over the interval $[\beta_{\min}, \beta_{\max}]$. Estimation is "fragile" if the range of inferences is large. Specifically, the result is designated as fragile if $[\beta_{\min}, \beta_{\max}]$ includes zero, and as robust if $[\beta_{\min}, \beta_{\max}]$ excludes zero.[1] Robustness and fragility in this sense are called L-robustness and L-fragility ("L" for Leamer) so as to distinguish them from other senses of robustness and fragility used below.

Some values of β in the range $[\beta_{\min}, \beta_{\max}]$ may fit the data very poorly relative to the unrestricted estimate $\hat{\beta}$. These values correspond to points in the parameter space that have very small likelihoods in terms of the observed data. To address this problem, Leamer and Leonard (1983, p. 311) propose restricting the extreme bounds to those points that lie within (e.g.) a 95% likelihood ellipsoid relative to $\hat{\beta}$. Cooley and LeRoy (1981) implement this modified EBA in their analysis of money demand equations. Granger and Uhlig (1990, 1992) propose a similar modification to EBA by limiting consideration to only those models with a sufficiently high R^2, relative to the R^2 of the unrestricted model.

McAleer and Veall (1989) criticize EBA for not accounting for the uncertainty in the extreme bounds estimates themselves. McAleer and Veall use bootstrap techniques to estimate the standard errors of the bounds and find that those standard errors can be large empirically. Magee (1990) derives the asymptotic variance of the extreme bounds:

$$\frac{ese(\hat{\beta})^2 + (\hat{\sigma}^2/\tilde{\sigma}^2)ese(\tilde{\beta})^2}{2} \quad \pm \quad \left[\frac{ese(\hat{\beta})^2 - (\hat{\sigma}^2/\tilde{\sigma}^2)ese(\tilde{\beta})^2}{qF_D} \right]^{1/2} \cdot \frac{\hat{\beta} - \tilde{\beta}}{2}, \quad (4)$$

---

[1] McAleer, Pagan, and Volker (1985, p. 297) denote this definition of fragility as Type B fragility; see also Leamer and Leonard (1983, p. 307). Other similar definitions of fragility in EBA also exist. However, the key results in Section 3 are unaffected by the particular definition chosen, so "Type B" fragility is used throughout as the definition of L-fragility.

where the two terms resulting from the "±" are the variances of the upper (+) and lower (−) bounds, denoted $ese(\beta_{\max})^2$ and $ese(\beta_{\min})^2$. As with the bounds in (3), the variances in (4) are calculable from standard regression output for the restricted and unrestricted models.

With the estimated bounds' uncertainty in mind, Levine and Renelt (1992) propose a modified EBA, which solves for "... the widest range of coefficient estimates on the [focus variable] that standard hypothesis tests do not reject" (p. 944). In practice, Levine and Renelt use 95% critical values for calculating the extreme bounds. If the variance of the estimate of β is insensitive to the linear combination of z_t chosen, Levine and Renelt's bounds are approximately:

$$[\beta_{\min} - 2ese(\beta_{\min}),\ \beta_{\max} + 2ese(\beta_{\max})]. \tag{5}$$

Thus, while pure EBA ignores the plausibility of the bounds (in terms of the data) and the uncertainty of the bounds themselves, computationally feasible solutions exist for addressing both shortcomings.

3 Implications of L-robustness and L-fragility

This section establishes that L-robustness is neither necessary nor sufficient for the data generation process (DGP) to be included as one of the models in extreme bounds analysis (Section 3.1). To simplify discussion, only the "pure" form of EBA is examined initially; the modifications to EBA are considered at the end of Section 3.1. A simple DGP and several classical regression models illustrate the four propositions associated with lack of necessity and lack of sufficiency (Section 3.2). In the examples, bounds are calculated at population values for the various estimates in equation (3). This permits a clearer exposition and in no way invalidates the results. In fact, the four propositions hold both in finite samples and asymptotically, and they are not restricted to the examples in Section 3.2. Hendry and Mizon (1990) provide the essential framework for this section's approach.

Other authors have also pointed out difficulties with EBA. McAleer, Pagan, and Volker (1985) show that the bounds may lie in implausible parts of the parameter space, that other information may be relevant to the model's usefulness (e.g., white-noise errors), and that L-robustness is sensitive to the choice of the parameter's prior mean and to its classification as free or doubtful. McAleer and Veall (1989) also show that accounting for the uncertainty in the estimated bounds can affect the results of EBA.

3.1 Four Propositions

L-robustness is neither necessary nor sufficient for the DGP to be included as one of the models in extreme bounds analysis. It is helpful to examine this statement as four separate propositions. No formal proofs need be given; the examples in Section 3.2 are sufficient.

Propositions 1 and 2 pertain to L-robustness.

Proposition 1 *If a set of models for EBA includes the DGP, a result may be L-robust.*

Proposition 2 *If a set of models for EBA excludes the DGP, a result may be L-robust.*

Propositions 1 and 2 are unsurprising. Still, together they imply that L-robustness says nothing about whether any of the models in the EBA are the DGP, and so says nothing about how close or far away any of the models in the EBA are to the DGP.

Propositions 3 and 4 pertain to L-fragility, or the lack of L-robustness.

Proposition 3 *If a set of models for EBA includes the DGP, a result may be L-fragile.*

From the perspective of an empirical modeler, Proposition 3 is problematic: correct specification of the unrestricted model does not ensure L-robustness.

Proposition 4 *If a set of models for EBA excludes the DGP, a result may be L-fragile.*

Propositions 3 and 4 together imply that L-fragility says nothing about whether any of the models in the EBA are the DGP, paralleling the implication about L-robustness from Propositions 1 and 2.

Propositions 1–4 extend immediately to EBA that is modified to account for uncertainty in the estimated bounds. For Propositions 1 and 2, a large enough sample size always exists such that the uncertainty in the estimated bounds is negligible. For Propositions 3 and 4, the results remain L-fragile when accounting for uncertainty in the estimated bounds because that uncertainty must increase the range spanned by the bounds.

Propositions 1 and 2 also extend to EBA that is restricted to lie within a likelihood ellipsoid, as when the doubtful variable has no explanatory power; see Examples 1 and 2 below. Section 5 discusses implications for Propositions 3 and 4.

3.2 Four Examples

Examples 1, 2, 3, and 4 below illustrate Propositions 1, 2, 3, and 4 respectively. A simple framework is used to characterize the implications as clearly and directly as possible.

Suppose that the data $(y_t, \ t = 1, \ldots, T)$ are generated by the conditional process:

$$y_t \quad = \quad \alpha_1 w_{1t} + \alpha_2 w_{2t} + \alpha_3 w_{3t} + e_t \qquad e_t \sim IN(0, \sigma_e^2); \tag{6}$$

and that the marginal variables $(w_{1t}, w_{2t}, w_{3t}) \ (= w_t')$ are normal, independent, and identically distributed:

$$w_t \sim IN(0, \tau), \tag{7}$$

where τ is the variance-covariance matrix of w_t. The dependent variable in (6) is the same as that in (2). For simplicity, τ is an identity matrix and σ_e^2 is unity, unless otherwise stated.

To evaluate the properties of EBA, the right-hand side variables in the conditional process (6) must be mapped into focus, free, and doubtful variables. Also, it is possible that some w_{it} may be omitted from all models in the EBA. In Examples 1–4, w_{1t} is the focus variable and is also the only free variable, w_{2t} is the doubtful variable, and w_{3t} is excluded from all models in the EBA. Thus, in these examples, only two models need to be estimated in order to calculate the bounds in equation (3) and the asymptotic variance of the bounds in equation (4). One model is the unrestricted model, which has both w_{1t} and w_{2t} as regressors. The other model is the restricted model, which has w_{1t} as its only regressor.

The EBA will satisfy any of Propositions 1–4, depending upon the values of the parameters in the DGP (6)–(7). Thus, the examples are stated in terms of the parameters of the DGP.

Example 1 illustrates Proposition 1.

Example 1 *Suppose that:*
  $\alpha_1 = 1$ *(the focus variable has a nonzero coefficient),*
  $\alpha_2 = 0$ *(the doubtful variable is unnecessary for explaining y_t), and*
  $\alpha_3 = 0$ *(the excluded variable is unnecessary for explaining y_t).*
  Then Proposition 1 holds for large enough T.

In Example 1, expectations of relevant estimators are $\mathcal{E}(\hat{\beta}) = \mathcal{E}(\tilde{\beta}) = \alpha_1$, $\mathcal{E}(\hat{\sigma}^2) = \mathcal{E}(\tilde{\sigma}^2) = \sigma_e^2$, and $\mathcal{E}(ese(\hat{\beta})^2) \approx \mathcal{E}(ese(\tilde{\beta})^2) \approx \sigma_e^2/T$, where the approximate equalities indicate evaluation at population values (i.e., the asymptotic approximation). These equalities imply that the term in square brackets in equation (3) is zero when evaluated at population values. Hence, the bounds are likely to be narrow in finite samples. For large enough T (or for small enough σ_e^2), the bounds can be arbitrarily narrow.

Example 2 is the same as Example 1 except that the omitted variable is important in the DGP.

Example 2 *Suppose that $\alpha_1 = 1$, $\alpha_2 = 0$, and $\alpha_3 = 1$. Then Proposition 2 holds.*

In Example 2, $\mathcal{E}(\hat{\beta}) = \mathcal{E}(\tilde{\beta}) = \alpha_1$, $\mathcal{E}(\hat{\sigma}^2) = \mathcal{E}(\tilde{\sigma}^2) = \sigma_e^2 + \alpha_3^2 \tau_{33}$, and $\mathcal{E}(ese(\hat{\beta})^2) \approx \mathcal{E}(ese(\tilde{\beta})^2) \approx (\sigma_e^2 + \alpha_3^2 \tau_{33})/T$. While these equalities differ from those in Example 1, they still imply that the term in square brackets in equation (3) is zero at population values. So, the bounds are again likely to be narrow, and they can be arbitrarily narrow for a large enough T. Worryingly, $\mathcal{E}(\hat{\beta}) = \mathcal{E}(\tilde{\beta}) \neq \alpha_1$ in general if w_{1t} and w_{3t} are correlated. That is, the restricted and unrestricted estimates have the same expectations, and both estimates are biased (and in fact are typically inconsistent) for the true parameter.

For the next two examples—Examples 3 and 4—the marginal process (7) is modified slightly to include a nonzero correlation (ρ_{12}) between w_{1t} and w_{2t}.

Example 3 *Suppose that $\alpha_1 = 1$, $\alpha_2 = -3$, $\alpha_3 = 0$, and $\rho_{12} = 0.5$. Then Proposition 3 holds for large enough T.*

Example 3 is the same as Example 1 except that the doubtful variable is necessary for explaining y_t, and the doubtful variable is correlated with the focus variable. In Example 3, $\mathcal{E}(\hat{\beta}) = \alpha_1$, $\mathcal{E}(\tilde{\beta}) \approx \alpha_1 + \rho_{12}\alpha_2$, $\mathcal{E}(\hat{\sigma}^2) = \sigma_e^2$, $\mathcal{E}(\tilde{\sigma}^2) \approx \sigma_e^2 + \alpha_2^2(1 - \rho_{12}^2) \equiv \sigma_r^2$, $\mathcal{E}(ese(\hat{\beta})^2) \approx \sigma_e^2/[T(1 - \rho_{12}^2)]$, and $\mathcal{E}(ese(\tilde{\beta})^2) \approx \sigma_r^2/T$. Further, F_D is a noncentral F-statistic, with $\mathcal{E}(F_D/T) \approx \alpha_2^2(1 - \rho_{12}^2)/\sigma_e^2$, which is essentially the noncentrality parameter divided by T. Thus, the extreme bounds are approximately:

$$\left(\alpha_1 + \frac{\rho_{12}\alpha_2}{2} \right) \quad \pm \quad \frac{|\rho_{12}\alpha_2|}{2}. \tag{8}$$

For the parameter values in Example 3, equation (8) implies extreme bounds of approximately $[-0.5, +1.0]$. In practice, the bounds may be even larger, noting that $\mathcal{E}(\hat{\beta}) = 1.0$ and $\mathcal{E}(\tilde{\beta}) \approx -0.5$. Even with these wide bounds, the unrestricted estimator $\hat{\beta}$ is unbiased for β; and, for (e.g.) $T = 100$, β is precisely estimated by $\hat{\beta}$, with an approximate estimated standard error of 0.12, implying a typical t-ratio of over eight.

The DGP in Example 4 is the same as in Example 3, except that α_3 is nonzero and so the unrestricted model for EBA does not include the DGP.

Example 4 *Suppose that $\alpha_1 = 1$, $\alpha_2 = -3$, $\alpha_3 = 1$, and $\rho_{12} = 0.5$. Then Proposition 4 holds.*

Because w_{3t} is independent of w_{1t} and w_{2t}, all results for Example 3 carry through, but with σ_e^2 redefined as $\sigma_e^2 + \alpha_3^2 \tau_{33}$.

7

4 An Empirical Example

To highlight the empirical consequences of the four propositions in Section 3, the current section re-examines an empirical model of narrow money demand in the United Kingdom from Hendry and Ericsson (1991). This model is described, and its history and properties summarized. Several alternatives to this model are then estimated, and extreme bounds are calculated for various model pairs. Treating the original model as the DGP, examples of all four propositions can be found empirically. Of course, the original model is *not* the DGP. However, that model does appear well-specified when examined with a wide range of diagnostic statistics, so it behaves like a local DGP, thus making these extreme bounds analyses of substantive interest.

The data are quarterly seasonally adjusted nominal M1 (M), real total final expenditure (TFE) at 1985 prices (I), the TFE deflator (P), and the net interest rate (R^*), which measures the opportunity cost of holding money. The net interest rate is the differential between the three-month local authority interest rate and the learning-adjusted retail sight-deposit interest rate. Equation (6) in Hendry and Ericsson (1991) is the following equilibrium correction model (EqCM):

$$\Delta(\widehat{m-p})_t = \underset{(0.004)}{0.023} - \underset{(0.125)}{0.687} \Delta p_t - \underset{(0.058)}{0.175} \Delta(m-p-i)_{t-1}$$

$$- \underset{(0.060)}{0.630} R_t^* - \underset{(0.009)}{0.093} (m-p-i)_{t-1}$$

$$T = 100 \ [1964(3)\text{--}1989(2)] \quad \hat{\sigma} = 1.313\% , \tag{9}$$

where variables in lowercase are in logarithms, Δ is the one-period difference operator, and estimated standard errors are in parentheses. Equation (9) is an empirically constant parsimonious simplification of an autoregressive distributed lag in the money demand variables. Equation (9) has long-run unit price and income elasticities but near-zero short-run ones; and the long-run interest rate elasticity is large and negative. Hendry and Ericsson (1991) discuss the economic and statistical merits of (9) in greater detail.

The history of (9) provides a perspective on its empirical validity, which motivates treating (9) as the DGP in the examples below. Hacche (1974) and Coghlan (1978) developed some of the first models of U.K. narrow money demand. Hendry (1979) noted problems in the dynamic specification of those models and obtained a better-specified model much like (9) as a simplification from an autoregressive distributed lag model on data through 1977. Equation (9) differs from Hendry's (1979) model by having the interest rate in levels rather than logs (a formulation proposed by Trundle (1982)), by having slightly simpler dynamics, and by having the net interest rate rather than the local authority rate. The net interest rate helps properly measure

8

the economic concept of the opportunity cost when narrow money started earning interest in the 1980s.

The empirical specification in (9) has been extensively analyzed. Aspects examined include parameter constancy [Hendry (1985), Hendry and Ericsson (1991)], cointegration [Johansen (1992), Hendry and Mizon (1993), Paruolo (1996)], weak exogeneity [Johansen (1992), Boswijk (1992)], super exogeneity [Cuthbertson (1988), Hendry (1988), Hendry and Ericsson (1991), Engle and Hendry (1993)], dynamic specification [Ericsson, Campos, and Tran (1990)], finite-sample biases in estimation [Kiviet and Phillips (1994)], and seasonality [Ericsson, Hendry, and Tran (1994)]. Only the last (seasonality) provides any evidence of mis-specification, and the magnitude of that mis-specification appears relatively small.

To illustrate the four propositions above, consider the following four variants on equation (9).

M_1 : equation (9) itself;

M_2 : equation (9), excluding Δp_t;

M_3 : equation (9), excluding Δp_t and $\Delta(m - p - i)_{t-1}$; and

M_4 : equation (9), excluding Δp_t and R_t^*.

Table 1 summarizes the estimation results for these four models.

For EBA, choices of excluded, free, doubtful, and focus variables must be made; and the following choices aim to illustrate Propositions 1–4. Treating M_1 as the DGP, the model pairs (M_1, M_2), (M_2, M_3), (M_1, M_4), and (M_2, M_4) correspond to Propositions 1, 2, 3, and 4 respectively in terms of whether the DGP is included in the EBA. Each model pair determines which (if any) variable the EBA excludes, relative to the DGP. For each model pair, the free variables are all of the variables included in the restricted model, and the doubtful variables are all variables excluded from the restricted model but included in the unrestricted model. The interest rate R_t^* is the focus variable for the first two model pairs, and the dynamic response to disequilibrium $\Delta(m - p - i)_{t-1}$ is the focus variable for the second two model pairs.

Table 2 presents the extreme bounds analysis for each of the four model pairs. The interest rate R_t^* is L-robust, whether or not M_1 is included in the models analyzed: see the first two columns of results. Conversely, the variable $\Delta(m - p - i)_{t-1}$ is L-fragile, whether or not M_1 is included: see the last two columns of results. Both variables are highly statistically significant in the original model M_1, with F-statistics of $F(1, 95) = 109.5$ $[p = 0.0\%]$ for R_t^*, $F(1, 95) = 9.06$ $[p = 0.3\%]$ for $\Delta(m - p - i)_{t-1}$, and $F(2, 95) = 55.97$ $[p = 0.0\%]$ for R_t^* and $\Delta(m - p - i)_{t-1}$ jointly.

To summarize, inclusion or exclusion of the DGP in the models examined has no bearing on the determination of L-robustness or L-fragility in extreme bounds analysis. Additionally, a coefficient can be highly statistically significant, yet be

Table 1: Estimates for Restricted and Unrestricted Models.

Variable or Statistic	Model			
	M_1	M_2	M_3	M_4
Δp_t	−0.687 (0.125)	–	–	–
$\Delta(m - p - i)_{t-1}$	−0.175 (0.058)	−0.133 (0.066)	–	0.343 (0.090)
R_t^*	−0.630 (0.060)	−0.786 (0.060)	−0.718 (0.051)	–
$(m - p - i)_{t-1}$	−0.093 (0.009)	−0.092 (0.010)	−0.084 (0.009)	−0.006 (0.012)
intercept	0.023 (0.004)	0.024 (0.005)	0.022 (0.005)	0.003 (0.007)
R^2	0.762	0.686	0.673	0.133
$\hat{\sigma}$	1.313%	1.498%	1.522%	2.478%
F-statistic vs. M_1	–	$F(1, 95)$ 30.01** [0.000]	$F(2, 95)$ 17.67** [0.000]	$F(2, 95)$ 125.3** [0.000]
F-statistic vs. M_2	–	–	$F(1, 96)$ 4.09* [0.046]	$F(1, 96)$ 169.3** [0.000]

Notes:

1. The dependent variable is $\Delta(m - p)_t$, and the sample period is 1964(3)–1989(2) [$T = 100$].

2. Estimated standard errors of coefficient estimates appear in parentheses.

3. In the last two rows, the three entries within a given block are the F-statistic with degrees of freedom as indicated, the value of that F-statistic, and the tail probability associated with that value of the F-statistic (in brackets).

4. A single asterisk * and two asterisks ** indicate rejection at the 5% and 1% levels respectively.

Table 2: Extreme Bounds Analysis of the Model Pairs (M_1, M_2), (M_2, M_3), (M_1, M_4), and (M_2, M_4).

Model pair	(M_1, M_2)	(M_2, M_3)	(M_1, M_4)	(M_2, M_4)
Proposition illustrated	1	2	3	4
Unrestricted model	M_1	M_2	M_1	M_2
Restricted model	M_2	M_3	M_4	M_4
DGP (M_1)	included	excluded	included	excluded
Focus variable	R_t^*	R_t^*	$\Delta(m-p-i)_{t-1}$	$\Delta(m-p-i)_{t-1}$
Bounds	$[-0.79, -0.63]$ (0.05) (0.06)	$[-0.79, -0.72]$ (0.06) (0.05)	$[-0.18, +0.34]$ (0.06) (0.05)	$[-0.13, +0.34]$ (0.07) (0.06)
Modified bounds	$[-0.89, -0.51]$	$[-0.91, -0.62]$	$[-0.29, +0.44]$	$[-0.26, +0.45]$
L-robust or L-fragile	L-robust	L-robust	L-fragile	L-fragile

Notes:

1. Even although M_1 is not the actual DGP, M_1 is treated as such to provide empirical examples of the four propositions.

2. Estimated asymptotic standard errors of bounds appear in parentheses underneath the bounds.

3. The modified bounds are calculated from equation (5).

either L-robust or L-fragile. As this section and the previous section show, these negative results are easily demonstrated in principle and in empirical practice.

5   Encompassing, EBA, and Robustness

This section interprets Propositions 1–4 in light of the encompassing literature (Section 5.1), relates Leamer and Leonard's modified EBA to encompassing (Section 5.2), and re-interprets several encompassing tests and diagnostic tests as tests of robustness (Section 5.3). See Mizon (1984), Mizon and Richard (1986), Hendry and Richard (1989), and Bontemps and Mizon (2003) for key references on encompassing.

5.1   An Encompassing Interpretation of EBA

Whether or not a variable is L-robust depends *inter alia* upon the correlations between the free and doubtful variables. That dependence leads to an encompassing interpretation of EBA. A simple regression model illustrates.

Returning to equations (1) and (2), consider the case with one focus variable x_t and one doubtful variable z_t:

$$y_t \;=\; \beta x_t + \gamma z_t + u_t. \tag{10}$$

With only one doubtful variable in (10), the extreme bounds are given by the unrestricted and restricted estimates $\hat{\beta}$ and $\tilde{\beta}$. The restricted estimate $\tilde{\beta}$ can be expressed in terms of the unrestricted estimate $\hat{\beta}$ as:

$$\tilde{\beta} \;=\; \hat{\beta} + (\textstyle\sum x_t^2)^{-1}(\textstyle\sum x_t z_t)\hat{\gamma}$$

$$\;=\; \hat{\beta} + r_{xz}\left(\frac{\sum z_t^2}{\sum x_t^2}\right)^{\frac{1}{2}} \hat{\gamma}\,, \tag{11}$$

where r_{xz} is the sample correlation between the focus variable and the doubtful variable. From (11), the distance between the bounds is the product of that correlation, the square root of the ratio of the regressors' sample second moments, and the unrestricted coefficient estimate for the doubtful variable. For similar interpretations, see McAleer, Pagan, and Volker (1985) and Breusch (1990).

Thus, for restricted models with statistically *invalid* restrictions, loose bounds (i.e., implying L-fragility) are unworrying. For example, for the model pair (M_2, M_4) in Table 2, the deletion of R_t^* switches the sign of the coefficient on $\Delta(m - p - i)_{t-1}$, resulting in L-fragility. However, the exclusion of R_t^* is statistically invalid; and the exclusion of R_t^* generates omitted variable bias in the estimation of β, where the

12

omitted variable bias is $\mathcal{E}(\tilde{\beta} - \hat{\beta})$, as from (11). The restricted model M_4 fails to parsimoniously encompass the more general model M_2 because R_t^* is statistically significant in M_2.

For restricted models with statistically *valid* restrictions, the restricted model parsimoniously encompasses the unrestricted model because those restrictions *are* statistically valid. If EBA obtains loose bounds in such a situation, those loose bounds must arise from the uncertainty in the estimated coefficients: the corresponding statistical reduction appears valid, implying no omitted variable bias.

The examples in the previous two paragraphs compare a given model with a more general, nesting model. A given model can also be compared with a non-nested model or with a more restricted model. Non-nested comparisons generate variance-encompassing and parameter-encompassing test statistics. General-to-specific comparisons generate the standard F-statistic, interpretable as a statistic for encompassing. On the latter, Gouriéroux and Monfort (1995, Proposition 8) demonstrate that (counterintuitively) a general model need not always encompass a model nested within it. However, Bontemps and Mizon (2003) find "... that the congruence of a model is a sufficient condition for it to nest and encompass a simplification (parametric or nonparametric) of itself, and that consequently [congruence] plays a crucial role in the application of the encompassing principle." (p. 355)

5.2   Encompassing, and Modified EBA

Leamer and Leonard's (1983) modified EBA restricts the bounds to lie within some specified likelihood ellipsoid relative to the unrestricted model. This statistical modification is very classical in nature: modified EBA considers only those models that are statistically valid simplifications of the unrestricted model. This modification is very much in the spirit of the encompassing literature, given the discussion in Section 5.1; and it motivates orthogonalization of variables in model design, as discussed below.

Equation (11) highlights an advantage to having nearly orthogonal regressors: they help minimize the potential for omitted variable bias. Because linear models are invariant to nonsingular linear transformations of the regressors, orthogonalization of the variables in the unrestricted model could be obtained by construction. For typical (i.e., highly autocorrelated) economic time series, near orthogonalization can often be obtained by using two economically interpretable transformations: differencing, and differentials. For example, in equation (9), inflation Δp_t is a differenced variable, lagged inverse velocity $(m - p - i)_{t-1}$ and the net interest rate R_t^* are differentials, and $\Delta(m - p - i)_{t-1}$ is a differenced differential. Transformation of the original level variables in the unrestricted autoregressive distributed lag into near-orthogonal variables in an equilibrium correction representation provides some insurance against omitted variable bias for the estimates in a restricted model, where the omitted variables are those variables that are deleted in the reduction from the unrestricted model to the restricted model. See Ericsson, Campos, and Tran (1990) for an example of such transformations and reductions with the U.K. money data.

While this sense of robustness is often achievable by design, no procedure appears capable of ensuring orthogonalization with respect to variables that are not included in the *unrestricted* model. This implication emphasizes the importance of starting with a general enough model. Leamer and Leonard (1983, p. 306) are sympathetic to this view, given their concern for obtaining robust inferences over a broad family of models. For detailed discussions of general-to-specific modeling and model design, see Hendry (1983), Hendry, Pagan, and Sargan (1984), Gilbert (1986), Spanos (1986), Ericsson, Campos, and Tran (1990), Mizon (1995), Hoover and Perez (1999), Hendry and Krolzig (1999, 2005), Campos, Ericsson, and Hendry (2005), and Doornik (2008).

5.3 Robustness and Encompassing

L-robustness focuses on how coefficient estimates alter as the information set for the model changes. From the discussion above, L-robustness is only statistically or economically interesting if the information that is excluded—relative to the unrestricted model—is *validly* excluded. Tests of encompassing are tests of that exclusion; hence tests of encompassing are interpretable as tests of robustness. Put slightly differently, an encompassing test of a given model evaluates whether or not the information in the *other* model is redundant, conditional on the information in the given model. If encompassing holds, then the given model is robust to that additional information.

At a more general level, robustness (and so encompassing) can be defined in terms of generic changes to the model's information set, and not just in terms of changes associated with the additional variables in another model; see Mizon (1995, pp. 121–122; 2008) and Lu and Mizon (1996). In a partition of information sources similar to the one in Hendry (1983) for test statistics, consider the following four sources of information: the model itself, other models, other sample periods, and other regimes.

Information from the model itself. Robustness to data in the model itself corresponds to satisfying a range of standard diagnostic tests, such as those for white-noise residuals and homoscedasticity. In this spirit, Edwards, Sams, and Yang (2006) propose a further refinement to Leamer and Leonard's modified EBA by requiring the bounds to satisfy not just the standard likelihood ratio test but also a battery of diagnostic tests. By focusing on congruence, this refinement parallels the generalized concept of encompassing.

Information from other models. Robustness to data in another model corresponds to standard encompassing: in particular, variance encompassing and parameter en-

14

compassing for non-nested models, and parsimonious encompassing for nested models. Differences in coefficient estimates across models are unimportant *per se*. Rather, the interest is in the ability of a given model to explain why other models obtain the results that they do. The formula for omitted variable bias provides one way for such an accounting. The relationship of the given model to the alternative model formally defines the type of encompassing statistic. Non-nested models generate variance-encompassing and parameter-encompassing statistics; nested models generate parsimonious-encompassing statistics.

If the two models differ in their dynamic specification, special attention must be given to the construction of the encompassing statistic, even although the comparison of models may appear conceptually equivalent to the one generating the usual encompassing statistics. See Hendry and Richard (1989) and Govaerts, Hendry, and Richard (1994) for details.

Encompassing accounts for information in other models. Model averaging is an alternative approach to accounting for such information. Early versions of model averaging include pre-test, Stein-rule, and shrinkage estimators; see Judge and Bock (1978). Raftery, Madigan, and Hoeting (1997) and Hansen (2007) exemplify recent directions in model averaging. While model averaging is an appealing way of combining information, it has several statistical disadvantages relative to encompassing through general-to-specific model selection; see Hoover and Perez (2004), Hendry and Krolzig (2005), and Hendry and Reade (2005) *inter alia*.

For example, consider model averaging across a set of models that includes a well-specified model (e.g., the DGP) and some mis-specified models. As Hendry and Reade (2005) demonstrate, typical rules for model averaging place too much weight on the mis-specified models, in effect mixing too much bad wine with too little good wine. Encompassing through general-to-specific modeling aims to find the well-specificd model among the set of models being considered, thus (to continue the analogy) singling out that one bottle of a rare vintage. If the union model is the DGP but none of the individual models are, the distinction between model averaging and encompassing is even sharper. Model averaging places zero weight on the DGP, whereas encompassing through general-to-specific modeling has power to detect the union model as the DGP.

Information from other sample periods. Robustness to data from another sample period corresponds to parameter constancy. Fisher's (1922) covariance statistic and Chow's (1960) prediction interval statistic are two early important statistics for testing this form of robustness. More recent developments have focused on testing robustness to a range of sample periods: see Brown, Durbin, and Evans (1975), Harvey (1981), and Doornik and Hendry (2007) *inter alia* on recursive statistics, and Andrews (1993) and Hansen (1992) on statistics for testing parameter instability when the breakpoint is unknown.

Information from other regimes. Robustness to regime changes corresponds to valid super exogeneity. Two common tests for super exogeneity are constructed as follows.

(i) Establish the constancy of the parameters in the conditional model and the nonconstancy of those in the marginal model; cf. Hendry (1988).

(ii) Having established (i), further develop the marginal model by including additional explanatory variables until the marginal model is empirically constant. Then, test for the significance of those additional variables when added to the conditional model. Insignificance in the conditional model demonstrates invariance of the conditional model's parameters to the changes in the marginal process; cf. Engle and Hendry (1993) for this test's initial implementation, Hendry and Santos (2006) for a version based on impulse saturation, and Hendry, Johansen, and Santos (2008) and Johansen and Nielsen (2008) for statistical underpinnings of the latter.

These tests use statistics for testing parameter constancy and statistics for omitted variables. Thus, these tests are interpretable as tests of robustness to information from other sample periods and from other models. However, tests of super exogeneity merit separate mention because super exogeneity is central to policy analysis.

Hendry and Ericsson (1991) calculate both types of super exogeneity tests. Hendry and Ericsson show that the EqCM (9) is empirically constant, but that autoregressive models for inflation and the net interest rate are not. The EqCM is constant across regime changes, which were responsible for the nonconstancy of the inflation and interest rate processes. From (i), inflation and the net interest rate are super exogenous in (9). Additionally, functions of the residuals from the marginal processes are insignificant when added to the EqCM, so inflation and the net interest rate are super exogenous from (ii). See Engle, Hendry, and Richard (1983) for a general discussion of exogeneity.

Overlapping sources of information. Robustness to the intersection of multiple sources of information is also of interest. For instance, robustness to another model's data over an out-of-sample period corresponds to forecast encompassing and forecast-model encompassing; see Chong and Hendry (1986), Lu and Mizon (1991), Ericsson (1992), and Ericsson and Marquez (1993). See also Bates and Granger (1969), Granger (1989), Wright (2003a, 2003b), Hendry and Clements (2004), Hendry and Reade (2006), and Castle, Fawcett, and Hendry (2008) *inter alia* for discussion on the related concept of forecast combination.

Other implications of encompassing. Encompassing does not imply that the DGP is included in the set of models being examined. However, an encompassing model is congruent with respect to the available information set and thus parsimoniously encompasses the local DGP. In that specific sense, the encompassing model establishes a closeness to the DGP. General-to-specific modeling with diagnostic testing enforces encompassing and generates a progressive research strategy that converges to the DGP in large samples; cf. White (1990) and Mizon (1995). Extreme bounds analysis—at least in its unmodified form—does neither.

6 Summary and Remarks

Extreme bounds analysis re-emphasizes the importance of robustness in empirical modeling. The measure of robustness in EBA has several unfortunate properties that render that particular measure useless in practice. Nonetheless, the structure of EBA helps elucidate an important role of encompassing and model design in empirical modeling: encompassing tests and several other diagnostic tests are interpretable as tests of a more appropriately defined notion of robustness.

References

Allen, S. D., and R. A. Connolly (1989) "Financial Market Effects on Aggregate Money Demand: A Bayesian Analysis", *Journal of Money, Credit, and Banking*, 21, 2, 158–175.

Andrews, D. W. K. (1993) "Tests for Parameter Instability and Structural Change with Unknown Change Point", *Econometrica*, 61, 4, 821–856.

Bates, J. M., and C. W. J. Granger (1969) "The Combination of Forecasts", *Operational Research Quarterly*, 20, 451–468.

Bjørnskov, C., A. Dreher, and J. A. V. Fischer (2008) "Cross-country Determinants of Life Satisfaction: Exploring Different Determinants Across Groups in Society", *Social Choice and Welfare*, 30, 1, 119–173.

Bontemps, C., and G. E. Mizon (2003) "Congruence and Encompassing", Chapter 15 in B. P. Stigum (ed.) *Econometrics and the Philosophy of Economics: Theory–Data Confrontations in Economics*, Princeton University Press, Princeton, 354–378.

Boswijk, H. P. (1992) *Cointegration, Identification and Exogeneity: Inference in Structural Error Correction Models*, Thesis Publishers, Amsterdam (Tinbergen Institute Research Series, No. 37).

Breusch, T. S. (1990) "Simplified Extreme Bounds", Chapter 3 in C. W. J. Granger (ed.) *Modelling Economic Series: Readings in Econometric Methodology*, Oxford University Press, Oxford, 72–81.

Brown, R. L., J. Durbin, and J. M. Evans (1975) "Techniques for Testing the Constancy of Regression Relationships over Time", *Journal of the Royal Statistical Society, Series B*, 37, 2, 149–163 (with discussion).

Campos, J., N. R. Ericsson, and D. F. Hendry (2005) "Introduction: *General-to-Specific Modelling*", in J. Campos, N. R. Ericsson, and D. F. Hendry (eds.) *General-to-Specific Modelling*, Volume I, Edward Elgar, Cheltenham, xi–xci.

Castle, J. L., N. W. P. Fawcett, and D. F. Hendry (2008) "Forecasting, Structural Breaks and Non-linearities", mimeo, Department of Economics, University of Oxford, Oxford, May.

Chong, Y. Y., and D. F. Hendry (1986) "Econometric Evaluation of Linear Macroeconomic Models", *Review of Economic Studies*, 53, 4, 671–690.

Chow, G. C. (1960) "Tests of Equality Between Sets of Coefficients in Two Linear Regressions", *Econometrica*, 28, 3, 591–605.

Coghlan, R. T. (1978) "A Transactions Demand for Money", *Bank of England Quarterly Bulletin*, 18, 1, 48–60.

Cooley, T. F., and S. F. LeRoy (1981) "Identification and Estimation of Money Demand", *American Economic Review*, 71, 5, 825–844.

Cuthbertson, K. (1988) "The Demand for M1: A Forward Looking Buffer Stock Model", *Oxford Economic Papers*, 40, 1, 110–131.

Doornik, J. A. (2008) "Autometrics", in J. L. Castle and N. Shephard (eds.) *The Methodology and Practice of Econometrics: A Festschrift in Honour of David F. Hendry*, Oxford University Press, Oxford, forthcoming.

Doornik, J. A., and D. F. Hendry (2007) *PcGive 12*, Timberlake Consultants Ltd, London (4 volumes).

Edwards, J. A., A. Sams, and B. Yang (2006) "A Refinement in the Specification of Empirical Macroeconomic Models as an Extension to the EBA Procedure", *Berkeley Electronic Journal of Macroeconomics: Topics in Macroeconomics*, 6, 2, 1–24.

Engle, R. F., and D. F. Hendry (1993) "Testing Super Exogeneity and Invariance in Regression Models", *Journal of Econometrics*, 56, 1/2, 119–139.

Engle, R. F., D. F. Hendry, and J.-F. Richard (1983) "Exogeneity", *Econometrica*, 51, 2, 277–304.

Ericsson, N. R. (1992) "Parameter Constancy, Mean Square Forecast Errors, and Measuring Forecast Performance: An Exposition, Extensions, and Illustration", *Journal of Policy Modeling*, 14, 4, 465–495.

Ericsson, N. R., J. Campos, and H.-A. Tran (1990) "PC-GIVE and David Hendry's Econometric Methodology", *Revista de Econometria*, 10, 1, 7–117.

Ericsson, N. R., D. F. Hendry, and H.-A. Tran (1994) "Cointegration, Seasonality, Encompassing, and the Demand for Money in the United Kingdom", Chapter 7 in C. P. Hargreaves (ed.) *Nonstationary Time Series Analysis and Cointegration*, Oxford University Press, Oxford, 179–224.

Ericsson, N. R., and J. Marquez (1993) "Encompassing the Forecasts of U.S. Trade Balance Models", *Review of Economics and Statistics*, 75, 1, 19–31.

Fisher, R. A. (1922) "The Goodness of Fit of Regression Formulae, and the Distribution of Regression Coefficients", *Journal of the Royal Statistical Society*, 85, 4, 597–612.

Freille, S., M. E. Haque, and R. Kneller (2007) "A Contribution to the Empirics of Press Freedom and Corruption", *European Journal of Political Economy*, 23, 4, 838–862.

Gilbert, C. L. (1986) "Professor Hendry's Econometric Methodology", *Oxford Bulletin of Economics and Statistics*, 48, 3, 283–307.

Goldfeld, S. M. (1976) "The Case of the Missing Money", *Brookings Papers on Economic Activity*, 1976, 3, 683–730 (with discussion).

Gouriéroux, C., and A. Monfort (1995) "Testing, Encompassing, and Simulating Dynamic Econometric Models", *Econometric Theory*, 11, 2, 195–228.

Govaerts, B., D. F. Hendry, and J.-F. Richard (1994) "Encompassing in Stationary Linear Dynamic Models", *Journal of Econometrics*, 63, 1, 245–270.

Granger, C. W. J. (1989) "Invited Review: Combining Forecasts—Twenty Years Later", *Journal of Forecasting*, 8, 167–173.

Granger, C. W. J., and H. F. Uhlig (1990) "Reasonable Extreme-bounds Analysis", *Journal of Econometrics*, 44, 1–2, 159–170.

Granger, C. W. J., and H. F. Uhlig (1992) "Erratum: Reasonable Extreme-bounds Analysis", *Journal of Econometrics*, 51, 1–2, 285–286.

Hacche, G. (1974) "The Demand for Money in the United Kingdom: Experience Since 1971", *Bank of England Quarterly Bulletin*, 14, 3, 284–305.

Hansen, B. E. (1992) "Tests for Parameter Instability in Regressions with I(1) Processes", *Journal of Business and Economic Statistics*, 10, 3, 321–335.

Hansen, B. E. (2007) "Least Squares Model Averaging", *Econometrica*, 75, 4, 1175–1189.

Harvey, A. C. (1981) *The Econometric Analysis of Time Series*, Philip Allan, Oxford.

Hendry, D. F. (1979) "Predictive Failure and Econometric Modelling in Macroeconomics: The Transactions Demand for Money", Chapter 9 in P. Ormerod (ed.) *Economic Modelling: Current Issues and Problems in Macroeconomic Modelling in the UK and the US*, Heinemann Education Books, London, 217–242.

Hendry, D. F. (1983) "Econometric Modelling: The 'Consumption Function' in Retrospect", *Scottish Journal of Political Economy*, 30, 3, 193–220.

Hendry, D. F. (1985) "Monetary Economic Myth and Econometric Reality", *Oxford Review of Economic Policy*, 1, 1, 72–84.

Hendry, D. F. (1988) "The Encompassing Implications of Feedback Versus Feedforward Mechanisms in Econometrics", *Oxford Economic Papers*, 40, 1, 132–149.

Hendry, D. F., and M. P. Clements (2004) "Pooling of Forecasts", *Econometrics Journal*, 7, 1, 1–31.

Hendry, D. F., and N. R. Ericsson (1991) "Modeling the Demand for Narrow Money in the United Kingdom and the United States", *European Economic Review*, 35, 4, 833–881 (with discussion).

Hendry, D. F., S. Johansen, and C. Santos (2008) "Automatic Selection of Indicators in a Fully Saturated Regression", *Computational Statistics*, 23, 2, 317–335, 337–339.

Hendry, D. F., and H.-M. Krolzig (1999) "Improving on 'Data Mining Reconsidered' by K. D. Hoover and S. J. Perez", *Econometrics Journal*, 2, 2, 202–219.

Hendry, D. F., and H.-M. Krolzig (2005) "The Properties of Automatic *Gets* Modelling", *Economic Journal*, 115, 502, C32–C61.

Hendry, D. F., and G. E. Mizon (1990) "Procrustean Econometrics: Or Stretching and Squeezing Data", Chapter 7 in C. W. J. Granger (ed.) *Modelling Economic Series: Readings in Econometric Methodology*, Oxford University Press, Oxford, 121–136.

Hendry, D. F., and G. E. Mizon (1993) "Evaluating Dynamic Econometric Models by Encompassing the VAR", Chapter 18 in P. C. B. Phillips (ed.) *Models, Methods, and Applications of Econometrics: Essays in Honor of A. R. Bergstrom*, Basil Blackwell, Cambridge, 272–300.

Hendry, D. F., A. Pagan, and J. D. Sargan (1984) "Dynamic Specification", Chapter 18 in Z. Griliches and M. D. Intriligator (eds.) *Handbook of Econometrics*, Volume 2, North-Holland, Amsterdam, 1023–1100.

Hendry, D. F., and J. J. Reade (2005) "Problems in Model Averaging with Dummy Variables", mimeo, Department of Economics, University of Oxford, Oxford, May.

Hendry, D. F., and J. J. Reade (2006) "Forecasting Using Model Averaging in the Presence of Structural Breaks", mimeo, Department of Economics, University of Oxford, Oxford, June.

Hendry, D. F., and J.-F. Richard (1989) "Recent Developments in the Theory of Encompassing", Chapter 12 in B. Cornet and H. Tulkens (eds.) *Contributions to Operations Research and Economics: The Twentieth Anniversary of CORE*, MIT Press, Cambridge, 393–440.

Hendry, D. F., and C. Santos (2006) "Automatic Tests of Super Exogeneity", mimeo, Department of Economics, University of Oxford, Oxford, February.

Hoover, K. D., and S. J. Perez (1999) "Data Mining Reconsidered: Encompassing and the General-to-specific Approach to Specification Search", *Econometrics Journal*, 2, 2, 167–191 (with discussion).

Hoover, K. D., and S. J. Perez (2004) "Truth and Robustness in Cross-country Growth Regressions", *Oxford Bulletin of Economics and Statistics*, 66, 5, 765–798.

Johansen, S. (1992) "Testing Weak Exogeneity and the Order of Cointegration in UK Money Demand Data", *Journal of Policy Modeling*, 14, 3, 313–334.

Johansen, S., and B. Nielsen (2008) "An Analysis of the Indicator Saturation Estimator as a Robust Regression Estimator", in J. L. Castle and N. Shephard (eds.) *The Methodology and Practice of Econometrics: A Festschrift in Honour of David F. Hendry*, Oxford University Press, Oxford, forthcoming.

Judge, G. G., and M. E. Bock (1978) *The Statistical Implications of Pre-test and Stein-rule Estimators in Econometrics*, North-Holland, Amsterdam.

Kiviet, J. F., and G. D. A. Phillips (1994) "Bias Assessment and Reduction in Linear Error-correction Models", *Journal of Econometrics*, 63, 1, 215–243.

Leamer, E. E. (1978) *Specification Searches: Ad Hoc Inference with Nonexperimental Data*, John Wiley, New York.

Leamer, E. E. (1983) "Let's Take the Con Out of Econometrics", *American Economic Review*, 73, 1, 31–43.

Leamer, E. E. (1985) "Sensitivity Analyses Would Help", *American Economic Review*, 75, 3, 308–313.

Leamer, E. E. (1997) "Revisiting Tobin's 1950 Study of Food Expenditure", *Journal of Applied Econometrics*, 12, 5, 533–553 (with discussion).

Leamer, E. E., and H. Leonard (1983) "Reporting the Fragility of Regression Estimates", *Review of Economics and Statistics*, 65, 2, 306–317.

Levine, R., and D. Renelt (1992) "A Sensitivity Analysis of Cross-country Growth Regressions", *American Economic Review*, 82, 4, 942–963.

Lu, M., and G. E. Mizon (1991) "Forecast Encompassing and Model Evaluation", Chapter 9 in P. Hackl and A. H. Westlund (eds.) *Economic Structural Change: Analysis and Forecasting*, Springer-Verlag, Berlin, 123–138.

Lu, M., and G. E. Mizon (1996) "The Encompassing Principle and Hypothesis Testing", *Econometric Theory*, 12, 5, 845–858.

Lucas, Jr., R. E. (1976) "Econometric Policy Evaluation: A Critique", in K. Brunner and A. H. Meltzer (eds.) *The Phillips Curve and Labor Markets*, North-Holland, Amsterdam, Carnegie–Rochester Conference Series on Public Policy, Volume 1, *Journal of Monetary Economics*, Supplement, 19–46 (with discussion).

Magee, L. (1990) "The Asymptotic Variance of Extreme Bounds", *Review of Economics and Statistics*, 72, 1, 182–184.

McAleer, M., A. Pagan, and P. A. Volker (1985) "What Will Take the Con Out of Econometrics?", *American Economic Review*, 75, 3, 293–307.

McAleer, M., and M. R. Veall (1989) "How Fragile Are Fragile Inferences? A Re-evaluation of the Deterrent Effect of Capital Punishment", *Review of Economics and Statistics*, 71, 1, 99–106.

Mizon, G. E. (1984) "The Encompassing Approach in Econometrics", Chapter 6 in D. F. Hendry and K. F. Wallis (eds.) *Econometrics and Quantitative Economics*, Basil Blackwell, Oxford, 135–172.

Mizon, G. E. (1995) "Progressive Modeling of Macroeconomic Time Series: The LSE Methodology", Chapter 4 in K. D. Hoover (ed.) *Macroeconometrics: Developments, Tensions, and Prospects*, Kluwer Academic Publishers, Boston, 107–170 (with discussion).

Mizon, G. E. (2008) "Encompassing", in S. N. Durlauf and L. E. Blume (eds.) *The New Palgrave Dictionary of Economics*, Palgrave Macmillan, New York, Second Edition.

Mizon, G. E., and J.-F. Richard (1986) "The Encompassing Principle and its Application to Testing Non-nested Hypotheses", *Econometrica*, 54, 3, 657–678.

Paruolo, P. (1996) "On the Determination of Integration Indices in I(2) Systems", *Journal of Econometrics*, 72, 1/2, 313–356.

Raftery, A. E., D. Madigan, and J. A. Hoeting (1997) "Bayesian Model Averaging for Linear Regression Models", *Journal of the American Statistical Association*, 92, 437, 179–191.

Sala-i-Martin, X. X. (1997) "I Just Ran Two Million Regressions", *American Economic Review*, 87, 2, 178–183.

Serra, D. (2006) "Empirical Determinants of Corruption: A Sensitivity Analysis", *Public Choice*, 126, 1–2, 225–256.

Spanos, A. (1986) *Statistical Foundations of Econometric Modelling*, Cambridge University Press, Cambridge.

Stewart, M. B. (1984) "Significance Tests in the Presence of Model Uncertainty and Specification Search", *Economics Letters*, 16, 3–4, 309–313.

Trundle, J. M. (1982) "The Demand for M1 in the UK", mimeo, Bank of England, London.

White, H. (1990) "A Consistent Model Selection Procedure Based on m-testing", Chapter 16 in C. W. J. Granger (ed.) *Modelling Economic Series: Readings in Econometric Methodology*, Oxford University Press, Oxford, 369–383.

Wright, J. H. (2003a) "Bayesian Model Averaging and Exchange Rate Forecasts", International Finance Discussion Paper No. 779, Board of Governors of the Federal Reserve System, Washington, D.C., September.

Wright, J. H. (2003b) "Forecasting U.S. Inflation by Bayesian Model Averaging", International Finance Discussion Paper No. 780, Board of Governors of the Federal Reserve System, Washington, D.C., September.